who *death*
made me

who *death* made me

Graphics Provided by:
Designed by: Hey Sunny Studio

ISBN: 9798376285626

"I started my life with a single absolute: that the world was mine to shape in the image of my highest values and never to be given up to a lesser standard, no matter how long or hard the struggle."

- Ayn Rand, Atlas Shrugged

who *death* made me

This is for those of you who have felt the cold, gnarled hands of death grip your life and ripple the course of your path in ways you did not ever imagine.

The words you find here are the valleys and peaks of the deepest heartbreak, the navigation through a forest of healing and the final set down of the earth held upon shoulders for far too long.

My hope is a sharp intake of breath as you turn the first pages,
And a dramatic sigh of relief as you close the last.

cheryl floris

contents

who *death* made me

who *death* made me

cheryl floris

cheryl floris

buried

who *death* made me

At 18 I walked up to the podium
400 people in front, eyes wide, thirsty for the words that would
stumble out my mouth
my aunt held me while I told a story about him,
what I thought his life was and who I thought he was
I don't remember a single word I said
at 18 I knew him as a different man
my words would be different now
all words seem different now
my world is different now

We toasted the man who was great
cracked a beer on stage during a funeral
and chugged that motherfucker back

You were the foundation,
Built strong walls,
Stable footing.

Although it came
Crashing down,
I remember you raised me.

— Strong base

who *death* made me

When I looked at you I saw a,
toad,
swollen, yellow, marked up and
empty.

But you weren't meant to swallow flies.

So i picked up my heart,
closed your lid,
and tried to erase that memory.

               — Why the fuck do they do final viewings

cheryl floris

You should have stuck
together after your
Dad died

                              I tried, but I
                              got tired of
                              picking up
                               pieces, of
                              others turning them
                               into lies
                              that
                              everyone
                              believed and
                              I became the
                              bad guy at 18
                              only because
                              I was trying
                              to do what
                              you told me to

                              Fill his shoes.

You could write
a book, they say.
I nod, thinking of
all the pain no
body sees as i try
(tried) my damn
hardest to take
the high road,
while they were
all chipping at
me.
Yes, I could,
I replied.
And you'd be in it, everyone
whose made their mark on my
memories,
my heart, my spirit.
Some may not want
to hear it, all the pain
they caused because
I chose to turn my
face to the sun,
welcome the challenge,
then move on.

cheryl floris

We used to sit on
the dock casting
lines,
no track of time,
shared beers in
the evening sun
of summer

We moved to a trailer, in the woods on the river and we donated all
of our possessions
until we had but a cast pan and pillows too flat
I thought that stripping myself of these worldly possessions would
strip away pieces of me until only pieces of my soul remained.
Exposed
I bathed in the river, scrubbed at my skin praying the ice water
would wash the sludge of darkness that lingered
The fire would burn the anger inside
Smoke would cleanse this broken spirit
Until I was bare through
And through
And through

You came to me
in a dream after
you died,
silent behind
everyone's eyes.
In your khaki
cargo shorts
you waved and
walked into
stardust and
then i knew
that you were
alright.

You clawed at me,
tore new wounds from the old.
I got tired of silently licking them closed,
and instead rubbed salt in them and
went to battle.

cheryl floris

There are days I can't remember your laugh,

                         Boston comes on the radio.

How far did your smile reach?

                         The lake is smooth as glass

Why can't I remember your smell

                         I pull into the garage.

— memories of a legacy

Was it peaceful as you went with
soft light and sweet memories as you
lie there hardly able to breathe?
Did you feel the hands reach
down/reach up and grasp ahold
of your soul? Was it gentle
and did you think of me
or the rest of your family as the
lights went out for the final time?
Will you be there waiting when my
day comes, will you
be the one to call me home?
Tell me
was it peaceful or
was it ugly?

In the sweet silence of daybreak I realized
this is what wildflowers feel when they are ripped from the earth

They threw the world of a 55 year old man at me. Bare it, they said, the other two can't, they said. So I dug in my heels, pulled up my sleeves, bore the weight of the earth on my shoulders and watched my childhood fall, at my feet.

— I didn't want to be atlas.

cheryl floris

Now i sit in
rows of flowers
wondering what
you look like in
your pine box,
wondering why
people think it's
beautiful to
preserve someone
who is already dead,
why don't we return
them to the earth
instead.

who *death* made me

My head is filled
with water unmoved,
the kind that becomes
stale and old
and oh how i
need it to move
so i turn on
Jimmy Buffet
and think of
you while
this water pours
from my head

cheryl floris

Somedays my heart freezes over
and I have nothing but anger inside,
burning sharp and burning bright
there is lingering shards of pain that remind
me you
are not here and
she is mostly gone so I am
alone

who *death* made me

Frustration starts to bubble and foam inside this chest
With a head this full, my thoughts must start oozing out of my ears,
spilling and tumbling down these shoulders,
Onto the the floor you used to tread.

With a head this full I toil over all there is to do,
Never ending.
Mine and yours,
The pressure others put on me,
To pick up where you left off.

And how dare you.

— *leave*

It was wilderness I didn't know,
trees I couldn't recognize
I stumbled along the path,
having smoked too much weed and drank too much drink
the world thumped and pulsed and I was lost in ways that I
couldn't find
there was no place to go but more to consume so I did
and this heart howled at the moon

who *death* made me

I'll plant daisies on your grave,
sow the seeds deep enough so you can
reach up and grasp the roots

Hold on to parts of me
your first born
your wife

When the daisies grow
I'll make a bed of them
knowing you're holding them and
holding me

Just don't ever let go

cheryl floris

And on the first day of summer
sunny summer
my world turned black
from a woman in uniform
who said you'd never come back.

who *death* made me

I'd dream a little dream
as I sat on this machine

The hum of the snowmobile clearing my head

We'd cross rivers and lakes,
fields full of deer,
find secret places only *we* could see and feel

The stars would dance,
as we took our turns,
they'd lead us home,
along with the hum.

I will allow myself to fall,
to feel.

I will allow this heart to break
open, not apart.

I will allow myself to listen,
to trust.

That there is a reason you left

      and allowed us all
            to crumble.

I was buried in grief
when you found me.

Inside an elevator as the
sun was rising.

Warm for march,
you held my heart and
gave me the first sip of true joy,

that I hadn't felt since the passing.

cheryl floris

I thought my mother would
hold me
when my father died,
but instead she turned
stone cold.

who *death* made me

I didn't have the chance to pack away your things / she went in, hot as a coal, heart just as black / packed up your things / "good riddance to that!" / in black garbage bags like your life/ presence / could be hauled out to the donation store just like that / all i wanted was your yellow shirt , the one i got for you when i was 12 / fathers day/ at the SAAN store / but the store is closed / your chapter too / I guess memories will have to do

26

cheryl floris

I am the hawk in the sky
circling in the afternoon high heat
spirit unable to fly high enough
away from the pain life seeks

who *death* made me

Flowers fill the tiny spaces of my home
trying to seep into the hole of my heart
and I wonder - why bring such beauty during a time of hurt

to help rid death from my nose

Silence breaks against the dawn,
and as I rise,
like an oak,
I know i can weather the
approaching storm.

who *death* made me

You felt like freedom, with
sunshine in your spirit and a
soul with no bounds. Oh how I
wanted to drive this old highway and
leave this town.

— Caught up

cheryl floris

who *death* made me

the lost years

I write to bring back
pieces of me,
the ones lost to long
ago memories.
Sometimes it's like picking up
tiny nettles from a spruce tree.

It'd be easier to set it
on fire.

cheryl floris

I watch the boards
rot
spider webs fill corners,
cupboards break,
dust collect,
useless things piles up,
and my heart
shadows over

— My childhood home is collapsing,
while they stand and watch

who *death* made me

Can you blame me for leaving?

The day we buried my father
my sister was being coddled
and I was being told I needed to
fill his shoes.

36

All I wanted was to be
embraced by you but
when I put my arms
around you I was hugging
a

                              statue

who *death* made me

At times i don't know
how to share the
pain
of my days.
I fear sounding
needy,
complainey,
and attention grabbing.
But the truth is
I am hurt and hurting
and I don't know how to heal

Death creeps into the
corners of my years
looms in my
peripheral vision,
waits for the
moment he can shake
my hand again

Flip flops in march didn't make sense,
neither did being in love with
2 people at the same time.

cheryl floris

I didn't know a
mother could hurt
her daughter just
so.
Little did I know
you were a wildfire,
waiting to be fed,
to grow.

— Standing up is gasoline

who *death* made me

I think empty
flowers pots are
filled with pain,
no longer useful, dug up,
you treat me the same.

cheryl floris

We were both
caught in the pain
of losing a
mother,
father,
tragedy brought
us together and
it felt like gravity
pulling our lives close
to help heal each
others wounds.

who *death* made me

I was shouted at and blamed,
dragged through the mud and on the brink
of insanity, but instead of burying who i
was i buried the relationships
those chose to wreck just like i
buried my father
and those wonder why it's not been the
same since an apology was made
but dear,
you can't get back something that's dead

'What he would have wanted'
they said, trying to threaten me like they
pulled the words from this head.

who *death* made me

I lost all of my people over
a
 truth nobody cared to know,
but I learned to get on just fine by myself,
and honour the honesty only I carried with me.

cheryl floris

I found a hole in
your heart where
love for me should have
been,
how silly to think
I was a flower
in your garden,

really I was just a
weed

who *death* made me

Death causes a
split in paths,
where you can
grow to the sun,
or you can drown
in the darkness

— So I turn my face to the east

Mountains were made
and forests were formed
not to navigate, not to explore
but to block out and keep in
for this broken heart
couldn't taken anymore

who *death* made me

Free yourself from the damage
that's been caused by this heart of mine.
I am not a good person after all.

How is she - they all ask
every time with the same reply that she's
doing her best
not wanting to reveal the pain that she's
in and the
pain that she's caused or
how I feel on standby for the final
call or
door knock from the uniformed officer
telling me it's time to make funeral arrangements.

who *death* made me

He used to call me
Snickers

　　　　　"Because you're a nut bar"

Now they call me
Atlas

　　　　　"Because you have to look
　　　　　　　　after everything now."

cheryl floris

I bled at 12
and kept it from
my mother for years
because I knew she
wasn't my protector,
I wouldn't have
been made to feel
comfortable but
laughed at behind
closed doors.

We never spoke of
our emotions growing up,
instead used your
empty beer bottles,
wine or
cans
and spoke our feelings
inside,
tried to screw a cap on
and leave them aside
to be broken and maybe
let fill from my
chest.

I was 2.
Torn in loss and in findings.
At a crossroads between separate parts of my heart.
Instead of my spirit screaming which path I needed to take,
it was drunk on drink and too much drug to notice.

We let lies flood us and taint our history.
After the yelling and throwing of
peanut butter jars and peanut butter cups,
everyday items turned weapons because our
tongues couldn't lash hard enough.

Now the past is rewriting itself, filling in gaps
and holes that we didn't know existed.
And somehow it all seems okay, because the
playing field is now levelled and we both
have the ugly sides that we never wanted.

This world is not for
the faint of heart,
although we're taught
to be softer, more vulnerable.

Those who have been touched
by death, had a nasty finger
laid on their heart,
understand the pain life and
living can cause,
but choose to do it anyway

These are the days I miss them the most
the love and affection of a parent
ease of conversation
gentle laughter
but one is 6 feet under
and the other 6 bottles deep

Self-raising, independent at 18

All that I do is to be the best for her
a mother that I haven't exactly had
and a father I am without

There are two calls from my heart and
I wish one would give it a fucking rest
and get out of dodge.

who *death* made me

The deep silence of rest
what i'd like to feel in my head.

— winter

cheryl floris

Some days morning coffee is enough
but others I need whiskey, and on
those days I bury my feet in
the earth and drink the wind, hoping
it'll carry the pain from me.

People will ask about my mother,
trying to be empathetic and show
they care,
But no one likes an uncomfortable answer,
so she's doing her best I say,
to avoid the truth that I fear
death will come
knocking on my door

— Sooner than later

And at 15 I drank too much,
same as the years after. I learned
real young how fun it could be
and
how sharp a weapon

I shoved you as i
filled with rage,
tired of you thinking
you are the wildfire,
growing.
Your words no longer
burn me because
as you diminish, I grow.
the only difference is
I don't do this for
show.

— Self defence

cheryl floris

I tore your mother roots
from me the day you
threatened my
daughter.
I laughed when you
thought they could be
planted again

When silence
bothers this overactive
mind i don't know
whether i should
fill it
or burn it

cheryl floris

My village is empty,
nobody home.
I guess I'll do it all
on my own.

— again

Who were you before
the illness made you
this way?
Were you loving,
tender,
did you like to play?
How did the voices make
you this way?
Where is my mother,
why couldn't she
stay?

When i was
t h i r t e e n
on the softball
team we won
our game and
I asked for
ice cream but
you said
 n   o
and when i
asked why you
said because
you are too
f   a   t
already

What starts as a frog in my throat,
leads to a mind blocked and confused,
a heart that steels over,
at any wrong
thought or two.
The sun beats on me, trying to melt what's welded shut, but I turn
my face to the wind,
how do I make my words easier to breathe?

We were strangers
in hallways, for
voices hadn't yet
speaked. Universes
collided when the
elevator doors
squeaked open.
Who would have
thought you'd
help me heal.

You had dark hair and spoke
with honey on your lips but
that doesn't mean you were sweet.

You were a sunbeam
Dripping your liquid sunshine
Onto me and this heart so blackened
By death
God the reprieve to feel so freely
And forget the living for a month or two
Even if my edges were being burnt
By you

Back then did you love me,
when I was nineteen and
deep in hurt I didn't realize I had.
When i was so broken and yet
you still cared.
Back then did you love me,
when we drove the city in your truck
and didn't say a word, all we had
was my hand in yours and the lights
to shine upon the signs that guided us
to our rooms.
Back then did you love me,
or was it a brief chapter that ought to
close.

cheryl floris

Death watches over us,
patiently awaiting his turn
to reach out those gnarled
fingers and grasp ahold of
another life,
another soul

— But the time isn't yet

Here I am in the Wastelands,

waiting and hoping for you.

How silly of me to think
my heart is outside of me.

We fell hard,
and I don't mean in love.
I mean the fall of our trust,
loyalty,
and belief in one another.

Can we surmount the hills that lie ahead,
made for us to crawl through, over and up,
hopefully conquer.

Or have we broken too much for repair,
when we fell so hard.

Time slips away
I don't remember what's true
what's been twisted by my heart
and what's been rightfully forgotten

cheryl floris

There is solace in roads
that lead to unknown destinations.

I cringe when I look at a map,
let me drive this gravel until the road runs out of earth

Was there a
mother i once
knew?
Too young to
remember the
times of steady
and warm,
tempted by the
sweetness I return
to the hive looking
for the mother i
once knew,
only to be stung
from the queen.

cheryl floris

I long for your embrace,
your voice,
the smile on your face

I wish you were here,
in mind
not just your body.

I wish you were here in body, and mind

I'd like to imagine flowers growing out of you,
8ft under.

I'd like to imagine flowers overtaking the spaces in your
mind,
that don't seem to work as fine
as they once did.

Maybe that's why I grow flowers,
they give me hope for what you could be.

— Both

We were a story that shouldn't have been written but was,
wrapped in grief and escape and hearts too young. We
drove the streets, led by lights, like it was our own private
path. Two strangers in the city no one knew us by name.
Who knew fate would cause us so much pain.

     – diverged.

And these unsaid words sit in my chest like a fire,
Not one aflame, but one struggling to light.

Smouldering, waiting for the right amount of oxygen before it can
burn hot and fast,
out of this chest
up my throat
and across these lips you used to kiss,
so sweetly.

There is a weight on my tongue,
after the slightest misstep i take,
I worry i will never be good
enough for you.

A piece of me is stuck with you,
and I am caught up in feelings I don't know that are past or present,
why can't the past lie still,
Instead it continues to melt and expose itself again and again.
Maybe I loved you then,
maybe I loved you still.

It seems i've run out of words,
I'm empty of them, none in my head or in my
heart.

The silence is comforting.

cheryl floris

The sun still sets when hearts break
I guess that's the world reminding us that
though our pain feels big,
it's small in the grand scheme of things.

A reminder from the earth that we will continue
to move
and rest
and journey forward,
although our hearts hurt, the scars are reminders of how strong we
can be

And the sun allows us to renew each day

Some have emotions and thoughts so clear
their mind is a cloudless sky
and i can't help but wonder and maybe
desire what that's like because
there is a daily price I pay in
trying to feel a clear path of my life

Pick up the pieces of your heart,
stick them together, glue them back in place,
it will never be the same but,
you'll be better for it.

who *death* made me

My mind is a storm
memories toiling
thunder booming from
my lips
Lightning strikes from
my tongue

cheryl floris

Memories are cool drinks
for the heart,
quench my longing,
but please don't run out

Have we lost connection with ourselves
because we've lost it with nature.
We bring plants inside to make it okay
that we pull them from the ground like a
Fischer plucks pike from the lake.
We have to return to the earth and
sink our hands in the soil, to soak up the
dirt and the good stuff to clean ourselves
from the scum of the world.

cheryl floris

Maybe my hearts too hard
for your kind of loving.

Toughened from the sun,
shelled from the world,
protected after experience.

Maybe my heart's too hard
for your kind of loving.

And so maybe I
            should just let go.

I let the salt
sink in my wounds.

A bit of pain for the damage I caused.

I wander aimlessly through
blood soaked days,
searching for adventure i can
no longer take,
my heart is longing
my soul hungry,
to breathe in fire
and eat mountains
drink the dirt
and feel the sting of
pine needles scratching into me

Love waits for none
but it fights for the chosen few
we have scars on our hearts
our love isn't new

I feel it deep in my bones,
ancient magic between the two.
So when we fight, we fight like hell
but we make up in the same and renew

cheryl floris

When the snow blows in,
I'll follow suit.
The pieces of me that
Strive,
Work,
Grind,
And go,
Will be blanketed over,
Allowed to rest.

who *death* made me

What was it like to have a mother
with a tongue sweet like honey
whatever words poured out were candy

What was it like to have a mother
with a voice like a river
that carried away the parts that don't
belong, settled the ones that do

What was it like to have a mother
spirit opened like a flower,
a woman you can talk to

What was it like to have a mother
a pack leader,
taught you to howl at the moon

What was it like to have a mother
arms of vines to hold you
whenever you needed her to

What was it like to have a mother
butterfly ,
with grace she taught you how
to fly and be unique in this
big sky

— Questions for my friends

who *death* made me

What happens to unsaid words?

Do they sit in the soul and
get heavier with time?

Do they turn to knots,
burls on old oak trees?

Will it turn to illness
in this heart?

Tell me how to liberate
and grow wings from
my mind.

cheryl floris

We were in space
wondering if we'd be brought together,
or if we'll move further apart

who *death* made me

I can fight with
my words and my
hands all the same,
you were a fighter,
you made me this way

— No place like home

You haunt my dreams and I
wonder if i haunt yours too.

I can't help but wonder what's
become of us now.
A path never to be walked,
Overgrown in weeds,
Trying to be reclaimed by nature,
But there's still parts of me that
Want it cleared.
Not to walk, but to know it's there.

The fire won't light, again and again i've tried, stuffing more paper, wood curls and kindling in. The damper open, I light the brown paper, hoping like hell it'll catch, I haven't been able to get it started since you left. I blow on the little flames, coaxing them along with prayer, but knowing it won't take. Knowing it's purposeful, knowing the element is keeping itself from me.

I shake my head, look down at the ash on my jeans and hands.
I don't need any fire right now,
no spark or flame to keep mine ablaze,
lit and fighting.
I need deep dark, water to cleanse,
sage to calm,
gentle with clarity.

So keep your flame, my dear fire,
I understand why you've withheld.

— A little like ash.

cheryl floris

Maybe in more time you'll fade,
a memory turning to ash.
You were once ablaze in my life
a spark so bright how could
anyone feel but joy.

Through time, you started to diminish,
you fed others but not the first of your soul.

Now you're hardly a flicker.

Maybe in time you'll fade,
maybe you'll turn to ash.

who *death* made me

When will my heart melt, the protection it keeps in place from the deep pain you caused. I feel it, the steel resting in my chest, guarding the most important part of me. Will it fall one day, or will it forever remain.

Wildflowers and cut flowers
My heart is at war
Life is unruly and I crave control
As I bury my hands in the dark earth
Trying to tame the chaos
Within me

You were the one I could trust to
hold me without crushing these fragile bones
that are so hard to find deep beneath the
armour that was built long ago

And now I'm building it up to block you out
the one who was never meant to hurt me

You think my
honey is sweet?

Oh just wait, it turns to
gasoline
the moment you use it
for yourself.

who *death* made me

I sit myself back,
clap the dirt and pine needles off my hands,
stare into the fire I just set ablaze
with the memories I wish not to have.

— Ash on my face

This path has so many questions,
hardest of all:
who do I love and
who do I let go

How frustrating it is when old emotions
resurface
breaking through the water to grab me,
after all the work i've done to lay them
to rest
how long will this fight be to keep
from dropping below the water line and
losing myself again

Maybe I will tear your page out of my book
crumple it up
throw it into the flames
I'll watch your place in my world get eaten by the fire
and hope your memories are burnt from my mind.

When my heart is at a crossroads I expect a demon looking for a deal
it should be a soul that did wrong and got trapped in hell.
Instead what I find is my shadow self trying to lead me astray from a life so
lovingly being lived

Your hands pressed valleys into my memories, I'm sorry I ever treated you this way. I lost love when I was eighteen, now I splash in puddles of rain trying to cover myself in all the love I've missed out on. But the puddles are dirt, my heart is too. Maybe I'm not worthy of loving you.

You became the temporary escape I so needed,
unknown to all but me,
a path that could have been walked,
but along it the flowers start to die
and the sky became unclear,
density is cruel,
with temptations that lead you astray.
I took a sharp left and discovered fields
of flowers in bloom and realized an escape becomes
tainted once reality sets in.

You grabbed me by
the scuff of my neck
tossed me aside
wolf mother tired of
trying with a sickness
fogging your brain
so i ran and i
became the wolf
that you feared
I'd be,
the woman
you could never have raised

I looked at her as i
put on my armour
and thought
how nice it must be
to be held with gentle hands
for all your years.
Then i cinched my
steel tight and prepared
to take on more blows.

You were too
drunk
to come to my
wedding,
2 years after
your husband
died,
I walked myself
down the aisle,
knowing i didn't
have parents any longer

who *death* made me

The first drink of sunlight eases
the steel over my heart and as the
Armour slips and exposes hidden parts of me
 I can't help but wonder what those who
have no barricades blanketing their heart
feel like

You can never demote
a mom from being
a mother but a
 mother can stay a
Mother all the same.
Some mothers you
just call by their
first name

who *death* made me

I fear waking up when I am older
5 10 20 years,
and I won't remember the small moments
like I should because this society has
us so distracted and I am
disgusted
that I have claim to these ways

cheryl floris

I've been mothering
myself since the day
I became a woman
not out of choice but
necessity ,
she was there but
there was no connection
so i guess i've figured
it out on my own
like you aren't supposed to

I have my fathers shoes
filled at 25
and when I glance around
at others living their lives
I realized i was robbed

You lap up attention
Like a thirsty dog trying to
Drink the ocean
But really you are draining the bowl

I realized my chapter
was closing when i
stood alone at my
wedding.
My old life was closing behind me,
carrying with it
my friends and family.
I stood alone,
barefoot in the grass,
and felt the glass
of a life passed
break

You rob me of
my peace with
every

       "how are you"

message
and yet I can't
bring myself to
block you

who *death* made me

I looked to the moon in wonder
I looked to the sun in discovery
these entities I grew to rely on had ripped love out of me
the iciness of night cast its shadow
fire burned a hole in my chest

I patched me over, let the scab settle in
but what the earth wanted was for the light to come in

Shadow me over
Burn me up
Wash me in light
I am a forest fire
Basking in rebirth
Regrowth

I looked to the moon in wonder
I looked to the sun in discovery
Earth answered prayers I didn't know I had

I am a forest fire

cheryl floris

I looked at my mother with
echos in my head from others
saying that hopefully she's learned her
lesson
but her eyes are empty and I wonder if anyone is
home

This isn't the woman I knew.

I'm worried about you alone she said
I'll be okay, I need to keep my head
to see my mother because
unfortunately I am now the rock and the
director of a family torn apart
by alcohol and speed

cheryl floris

I am the forgotten friend
Never invited for outings or
coffee dates or hikes in the mountains,
but still good enough to vent to.
I will not have memories of my twenties or even
thirties of weekends with the girls, shared
secrets on pull out couches, bellies rumbling
full of laughter.
I will not be a bridesmaid or
Godmother or considered
aunt by any of my friends children.
I am the friend in your peripheral,
there but never in focus.
Fed with occasional words sweet enough
that I continue to hang on,
hoping, hoping,
that I will not be the forgotten friend
anymore.

Release it all, I don't want it
the wonder and division,
the words left unsaid,
bury it, burn it, leave it for dead,
rid it all from me
let history stay as it should.

I may have been in the middle,
stuck between 2,
but I was right in choosing,
the man who fought like you
didn't' do.

When day breaks and,
the sun starts to rise,
so will i.

When snow falls and
the world gets quiet,
so will i.

When spring arrives and
flowers begin to bloom,
so will i.

When the light changes and
darkness starts to approach,
I will embrace the shadow
sides of me,
while being guided by the
moon.

Instead of dancing to the slow songs,
drunk on love, we're dancing around the pain. Fearful of hurting
again and when
another broken promise will lay. But the
only way out of this is to sweep the glass
of our hearts from beneath our feet and plant
wildflowers to remind us of how soft love
can be

and how resilient too.

We moved so much
because i didn't know
where to be,
turns out home
is in me,
so i walk barefoot
in the grass and snow
trying to plant myself wherever
I go

cheryl floris

cheryl floris

healing // *healed*

who *death* made me

Give me back the songs
the spring sunshine drives
city lights
and pieces of my soul that are stuck in your past

Death burned through me
like a hot knife

In the beginning,
I turned from it
scared to face its devilish looks.

But then I let it
consume me
tear through me

And I was able to find life again.

—finding flowers

who *death* made me

At times I feel like you
spoke to her
and said

                Keep watch
                      over my baby,
                      guide her and

hold her heart
                  when she needs

because she is exactly,
who I hoped she'd be

Art is messy
and life should be too

Paint stained clothes become
memory stained years so please let go,
of the need to control and have the house in order because,

art is never in order
life isn't either.

All the faults of heart are but
my own
maybe one day a storm will roar in,
the thunder will clap free the grasp they
have on me.
And i'll finally know how it feels to remove
the guilt from the past version of me.

cheryl floris

I have mothered myself for years
and many more ahead
so when you ask

"why is she like that?"

I'll throw back my head
and laugh to the moon,

"Silly woman,
you were shown the way,
bread and butter in hand
you skipped down the lane
in your little dress being
led by the woman who was
so blessed to have you.

I went with axe in my hand,
left to cut my own trail.
I had to learn how to
set a snare and dresses
weren't practical for the work
lay ahead so i pulled up my
pants, got my hands
dirty and became my own
Mother in the end.

I learned after you died that
there wasn't many to count on
but you
and now instead of walking on
the earth you are
becoming a part of it and i guess that's
okay because
nature is everywhere
and so are you.

cheryl floris

I stopped seeking
your attention
when i realized
you never listened
when i spoke to
you

— uhuh

I was never taught
how to be a lady,
I learnt from movies
and books.
I know how to change
the top end on a snowmobile,
maintenance a chainsaw
and work like a dog.
I am just now,
learning,
how to put on a dress.

I watch my friends
with their mothers
and know i'll
never
have that with my own,
but i can choose
to be that mother
for my own.

— Breaking cycles

Each day I am stumped
as a parent,
I wonder
      "How did you lead?
      How did you teach?
      How did you provide
      Such memories?"

The answer will always
be heart
and wearing it and
watching it outside of you

At 2am when I awake,
the moon bathes its light, full.

As I watch it, watching me,
I know that you, too,
are watching over.

— Comfort

who *death* made me

I will find the streaks of sunshine in my home
to quietly sit and
sip my morning coffee

cheryl floris

I'll spend days pawing at the pain,
trying to rid it, to go away,
but all i really need
is the sharp cold of the lake
to wash the filth of my past from me
and remind me
I am human

who *death* made me

I'll write these words on a piece of paper
burn them in a fire like they say to do,
when the moon is new,
because I don't want you, to be stuck in my
soul or heart or throat.

Instead of these words passing my lips
I'll burn them from the inside so they are out of me
and no longer tied to you

cheryl floris

I've spent these years
ripping off band aids
of all the pain caused
and the loss
and the heavy
burden on my
shoulders, now
shrugged off and
I've found flowers
growing beneath the weight,
baby's breath and daisies
out of all my scars.

You carved caverns in
me but your
love made the flowers
grow so i guess i should
say thank you for

Making me who i am

If i could bottle up the way
you smelled
it would be 2 stroke in the winter.
Now my husband wears it and it
suits him just fine

— You would love him

cheryl floris

If birds can call to each other why can't you and i/ we are the same you see/ your blood is in me/ your eyes are mine/ the way my lips creep across my face as i smile or grimace/ that's all you/ i have roughness on my hands from the hard work i learnt from a man who shares the same blood as me/ maybe i don't need to call because you're in me / after all these years and tears and missing you / so all i need to do is look in the mirror / all i need to do is smile and laugh/ you call to me everyday because i'm me/ we're really as close as that

I find my reprieve
in turning my face
to the sun and
allowing its spring
warmth to crack
the hardness that
winter forms

You were a version of good but
not my version of good and
that meant you weren't for me
But that's okay because my
heart is home and exactly
where it should be.

The wind whips at me, through me
Sharp as ice and,
Reminds me that I'm alive.

The sun crests the tree line,
Caresses me sweetly and,
Reminds me that I'm alive.

The crunch of snow under my bare feet,
Shocks my nervous system and,
Reminds me that I'm alive.

In the dead of winter, when the world sleeps,
My soul seeks out ways to drink in life.

As I breathe in, and the cool air catches my breath,
I can't help but find joy in the difficulty of such a menial thing.

cheryl floris

We were a home of
tight lips, stiff hips,
armoured hearts
and spirits that
couldn't part with
all of the tragedy of
past days and years.
I was child, unknown
to what living meant
and what loving felt
so when you died i
yelled and poured emotion
from my soul,
heart exploding to the
kind of living life had
and only now do i understand
the power of dance and
letting go of tragedy so
that i can grow

who *death* made me

I have a plaid
jacket that's 3 generations
old, with patches and
worn out cuffs, some
buttons no longer
do up.
It's carried pack
of smokes in the
pockets, i'm sure
a couple cans of beer,
the occasional joint
or two.
It's seen campfires,
wood getting days,
walks to neighbours;
babies have been
kept sheltered in
this coat.
I don't know if
it's ever been washed,
and i worry that'll
take the
memories away.

The grandest
moments of my
life has been
both big and small.
Birthing
and
the smell of coffee
at 5m with
the man i spend
the rest of my days
with.
The small is only
insignificant if we allow it to be.
Choose what burns
into your
memories

who *death* made me

Time melts through
my fingers like
bubblegum ice cream
on a too hot day
and i wonder who
I can pay to give me
more

They say love
has no bounds,
but i think
that's inappropriate.
I think love
needs bounds in
certain manners.
I think love
needs to learn
respect, understanding.
We are the ones
who shape those bounds.
Sometimes it takes
time and wrong turns
to allow them to find
their place.
Sometimes there is
pain and heartache.
But there is joy and
comfort when it is
found.
There is peace
in loving bounds.

They chuckled at
us getting married,
too young to know what to do,
but they didn't understand
what we'd been through,
they didn't understand that
death marries you

These words consume me but,
they're better off unsaid, and
I'll do my best to breathe them
into the wind, be carried off,
out of me instead.

who *death* made me

My heart calls but,
the cry is unclear,
and I search for the answer,
in the trees and under bushes
and in the rays of the sun that
tries to penetrate this armour
and once i'm exhausted of looking
I lay my head down at night
and the answer is in the eyes of my lover.

Every chapter I've turned
new section of
my life
I've worked through
riddled with
pain
heartbreak
hope
happiness
difficulty
has bred this resilient soul that I
now possess

Day breaks,
the sun falls,
I find comfort in the moon as she rises.

Let my dreams
float and grow
onwards and upwards to
better tomorrows.

cheryl floris

As I watch my friends share father-daughter dances,
I am no longer sad at moments missed but,
nostalgic for the moments not appreciated enough.

I only have well wishes for those to breathe in the small moments,
time passes so quickly,
we don't know when it will end.

who *death* made me

And here we are after the darkest time,
welcoming back the light

                                        — on love

"Your garden is thriving!
What's your secret?"
I ask

"I just plant things
where i feel the good
energy."

What a great motto for life.

Some days I am
in between
hurt and healing,
but when the grass
grows beneath my
feet as I take these
steps forward,
I know i am going to be okay

cheryl floris

She asks where you've gone
To heaven i say and she says
Well let's go there and play
It doesn't quite work like that love
What do you mean
It's a place we can't go, not yet, just
when our time is due, and sweetheart you're
still too new
but he's always with us,
you and Me, in our hearts
and the birds and the leftover cans
we see on the backgrounds, once held
by hands that were soaking up fun.
So for now we'll play here in our
home instead and find him in
the magic of the years ahead.

who *death* made me

Oh how we dream, of what
Could have been
Would have been

There are few certain things,
living and the knock of death
reliance on the sun rising and melting into the earth

and that there will always be morning coffee

Love changes as you age,
who'd know id have more scars on
this heart but love deeper despite all
the pain.

who *death* made me

I am alone but,
I am not lonely
I speak to my ancestors who've
come before me,
all the ones who have gone too soon

We speak with the sun
Laugh with the moon

Tell stories of similarities because
our paths are all the same
Some longer than others and
many full of pain

I journey forward with love and care
for those who help hold my soul
Knowing this is the last trip for a spirit
ancient as mine, as ours

For I am them and they are me
I am alone, but I am not lonely

cheryl floris

In the dawn of the day,
his love speaks volumes,
by the way he makes morning coffee.

Fingers in dirt,
as the sharp breeze stings my cheeks.
sunshine melts the snow and renews the hibernation of hope in my
heart.
It's too early, but the longing thrives.
To sink my hands into something that starts over each year.
Uncovering,
Revitalizing,
Sprouting.
Thaw these pieces of my soul.

cheryl floris

I am no longer in 'destination mode'

I have brushed hands with death one too many times in the last 8
years to not appreciate
every
ounce
of this journey I am on.

I fear for those and envy those
whose hearts have never been touched
by the dark, crisp hands of death himself.

To love life fully without pain in your heart may be freeing,
but fearful as well.

And yet, do they see colours as clearly as I do?
Is there appreciation in the wind or
how the birds scavenge the dead.

Is their life as fully loved and lived as mine is.

When my head lays on the bed of daisies,
and I hear my final bird call,
I will not fear death,
for I have known him, and will know him for the better part of my
life.

For the last
year I have
turned my face
to the sun.
A healing woman,
A hurt woman,
and I've watched myself
become who i am
meant to be

Darling don't hide your face from the
sun

Let her fill you up in ways only she
knows how

I dream of flowers and the
spaces they could fill,
in my house,
in my garden,
in my heart
and mind.
I too, can be this beautiful,
and resilient, and free to be
whatever I wish.
A mothers touch,
A dreamers mind,
A child of nature.

As the sun sinks below
and the clouds turn
grey

May you allow your soul to, as well

When the searching comes for the you,
you want to be

May you remember the skies clear too.

I am the healer with
Golden hair that your grandmother of
Generations past sent you to
With honey dripping from these lips
Onto the scars so blackened from neglect
We'll melt the scabs and bring
Flowers to plant in the cracks
Of the trauma from your past because
I am the healer with
Golden hair that your grandmother of
Generations past sent to you.

While my heart is in despair I must
remind myself that
I too, am like the tide,
with highs and lows.
But i'm the one who controls
them.

When death comes rapping at your window,
you'll notice many things change.
Values being one of them.
dream houses get smaller
adventure gets bigger,
at least - that's what I hope for you
Horns are grabbed
Doors are walked through
The desire to embrace life moves up on the priority list

And today I see my blonde children running out to the garden
Giggling along the way
I laid myself back, felt the crisp sun on my face and placed my
arms under my head.

I knew I made the right decision,
While my family craved a PhD and big house on the hill for my
future,
I craved more life.

There is nothing like
the sharp bite of
cool water on too
hot skin, is this
baptizing? The lake
ridding me of
sin. As i shallow
dive into a wave
on a summers night,
the water is in me,
on me, through me.
Quenching my fire,
 purifying my soul,
rooting me to me
and reminding what
It's like to
gasp for life.

The morning sky calls me,
stirs pieces of my heart I haven't touched for,
fear it may break. You see these
pieces are fragile and need delicate touch only
you can provide.

cheryl floris

The creases in my palms
are the women before me,
hands started smooth
and clear
have become worn
and used generation
after next
hands that tended
fire, babies,
men,
became idle and
clean once more.
Not shiny and pure,
empty and itching,
fear to answer the call anymore.

The creases in my palms
were idle for too long,
from my mother and
hers and now they
say my palms are
not 'lady like'
too rough,
grooves too deep,
but i'm here to remind them of
who we used to be

Somedays I am more lost than found
but I will continue to search for my path
and listen while it calls me home

Rain will come
and dampen your days.

Instead of trying to find shelter
from it,

Let it wash over you
and through you

Renew your bones
Freshen your soul
Blanket yourself in the wash.

Everything is greater after rainfall.

My dear,
do not lose the electricity of life,
the moments that you drink in sunshine
and feel the pull of a life lived so presently
you lose thought of anything that isn't happening right in front of
you.

The moments of in between when the
good and the great has already happened and
the visceral joy is explosive in the depths of your gut.

These are the times that will imprint on your memory to last until
the final day is done.

So fill your life with these moments,
pour another cup of liquid sunshine and
fill yourself with the electricity of life.

cheryl floris

I hope the mountains make you feel small
and the sky even smaller

I hope the trees make you feel young
and the earth even newer

Let them remind you that the problems
you face are small in this
world.

It is easier to pick yourself up, then it is to stay still.

Move with the wind

— Do not dwell

This soul is ancient,
digging rivers with the hammer it carries,
shaping mountains as it tracks with purpose across these lands,
reaching into the earth and feeding the soil with all that it's been
raped from.

And when the women approach and they are unclear, this soul will
bathe them in the iciest of waters and make them shed their skins
to expose the history of who they are.

And when the men approach and they are unclear, this soul will
send them into the depths of the forest to hew axe and cut wood,
to cycle the dirt from their pores and remember what it means to
be man.

cheryl floris

When the decision is to take from this ancient soul, you are deciding to be cast into the depths of the wasteland. There will be no way out but through.

If you're lucky, you will find the track in which this soul tread, and follow the steps through the mountains, across the rivers, against the winds, and into the heart of the forest so black it's blind.

Listen to the wind, and it will guide you. To the soul of light.

— Cailleach

I spent a lot of time wondering where you are,
heaven or Hell,
trapped in your pine box.

Now I spend that time, knowing you're safe,
and planning where I'm going.

I try to breathe
in motherhood,
sometimes i choke,
you were the one
I hoped to teach
me how,
           but i've always
been on my own,
I'll figure it out now

who *death* made me

You shaped me into who I am today,
Through all of the pain and lessons
I had to endure, thank you

— There is love in loss

cheryl floris

You said I had changed,
At 18 that felt like a splinter in my palm,
I would dig for it, try to figure out
How
When
Why
Into who?

You said that I changed,
At 25 that feels like the compliment I have earned
And one I will continue to welcome

I wondered why
I was never loved
the same as my
sister,
why did she get
a mother and
I a father?
Now i find comfort
knowing that i am
my own mother
raised by my father,
supported by the
Mothers around me.

cheryl floris

I need sunshine
and earthy air,
I've seen what happens
when you sit in a
chair an
do nothing your
whole life.

How did I turn my face from
this kind of love?
We burn hot like the stove that heats our home
and when the winter breeze sneaks through
the cracks of this old farm house, we work to
find the weak spots and we,
repair them

cheryl floris

In small towns names mean more.
Where half the street lights don't work
and the countertops are blue in the grocery store
you have conversation with the mom of the man who took your
virginity and
the guy at the bottle depot remembers when your dad died.
The school knows your history and you can point out the home of
your first grade teacher because she lives on that gravel road down
the back end of town by you

Names mean more because you may have gone
but you're not forgotten.
While the rest of the world moves on your,
memories are still pinned to the sidewalks and
the backroads and
the green space by the park
and I guess that's why we
keep coming back home.

I often think/ how many worlds shattered, shifted / upon the
passing of you / daughter of a wealthy man / a smart man /
a proud man / fate changed the course of my life/ as i
wander this path laid before me / i become the shaper of it

cheryl floris

When the sun starts to sink,
The swell settles
And my heart needs more space to grow

We created these days to give us more
And less, too

Goodbye to the day and the worldly possessions
That no long occupy

I'll sink into the sun and remember
        Remember
                Remember

When the day comes,
for me to crawl into a
bed of daisies of my own,
I will not shake hands
with death
but fall into its arms
like a warm embrace

We revelled in the nothing days,
kids gone wild while we danced in
the dining room of our too small
too stuffed house, chaos spilt around
in toys and baby socks and toddler
dresses, trying to laugh at the mess
knowing it would be gone too soon.

We hang a cow skull in our tree with
eyes intact and
tongue and
brain
like it's the most natural thing to do,
while others eat food from a factory and
balk at us like heathens but
who has really lost sense of this
world, the one who tries to bubble wrap it
or the one
who tries to become it.

There is something so
pure
in a simple life,
well lived.

House on a farm,
raising wild kids.

A mansion not needed,
fancy degrees, big accounts.

Just this little family,
chickens,
a garden,
and a few hounds.

— What he really wanted for me

who *death* made me

I will tear your page out of my book,
crumple it up,
throw it into the flames.

I'll watch your place in my world get eaten by the fire

And hope your memories are burnt from my mind.

cheryl floris

Some days I don't want to feel fresh
I want to feel made of earth
So I'll leave the dirt beneath my finger nails
Unwashed hair, tangled and riddled with twigs
Blackened soles from pacing the garden
And sunkissed skin

Judge all you want,
But we came from the earth and we are
Made of it
And we will return to it when our bodies break down
And bones turn to dust.
Why not feel like home for a short while.

It's okay to love
the birds and the
trees and give way
to any worry because
the days are pleasant
and the love is good
problems don't need
to arise out of the
recesses of your mind

cheryl floris

I am mountains
too tall
for you to climb,
valleys carved
too deep
by life,
lit ablaze
I am the hottest wildfire
you will see

You could never handle loving me.

who *death* made me

But he can,
he is the ocean,
my calming sea

He's taught me how
to take the hardest
parts of me and
magic them into
flowers,

into sweetpeas

cheryl floris

I want to
coat my life in
honey
grab the golden light
and drape it over
my life.
Watch it
       shimmer
       vibrate
       explode with crystals of love and
                   sugar i've never tasted

who *death* made me

I'll move with the phases of the moon,
and learn when it is time to shrink,
fade away,
embrace the dark.

And learn when it is time to grow,
fill up,
and light the world.

When the fire goes out of my wood heated house I feel the,
chill on my nose and fingertips

I wonder how long until we're warm again once the,
stove is lit and ablaze

Mind wanders to my children to ensure they are,
warm and calm

Then I remember it's not the house I should concern of because I am the,
home to these ones.

— warm mothering

who *death* made me

Through the woods and the bush and the tree,
snow ice cold, up to my knees,
I spotted your beauty, aways up ahead,
after I took the shot, lowered my head,
gave thanks to you, and all that you'll provide,
now I know, what it means
        to take a life.

cheryl floris

I was searching for the place where I belong
in worldly things, places and faces,
in the end home is me, as me
wild pieces and all.

I watch you grow,

Like the grass
and the trees.

I remember that they fall too.

cheryl floris

At 26 years old
I finally felt
what it was like
to feel pretty in a
dress.
That's a con you
see, to being raise
mostly by my father.
I lacked knowledge
and feeling of femininity.
But i'm starting to
find my balance of
working like a man
and
feeling like a woman.
This is another side
of healing.

I realized i was
healed
when i could
no longer write
about you.
Not even a line
Or two

I'll walk every inch of our land,
caress the trees, whisper sweet words,
sing melodies. My footprints will fall
on the grass so soft, trace my fingers
in the water. The flowers and I will
Talk.

– i'll marry the land.

What ever happened to those who like to burn shit, shoot shit and shoot the shit on a Saturday afternoon.
No cell phones, just laughter.
No drama, just fun.
A little rowdy, as we watch our kids play in the snow.
Connection under the sun.
Building community,
and the kinds of friends who stop by whenever for whatever.
"Let's just burn this whole thing!"
And we light the fire, we pass one around and we make memories.

Burning cabinets.

We are a unique breed,
those of us raised by strong fathers
and
broken mothers
and broken fathers
and strong mothers

We can withstand the storm.

I feel like all I
can write about
for my husband
is moments over
coffee, to some that's
silly , but to me it's
everything.
Campfire coffee,
5am coffee,
Post hike coffee,
Roadtrip coffee,
Afternoon 'i probably shouldn't have this' coffee.

I think coffee
is just a marker
of the moments where
we have our deepest
 connection and in
that case -
I'll have another cup.

I will teach my daughter
how to
plant flowers,
bake bread for
Sunday mornings
and love from the heart.
I will teach my daughter
how to
set boundaries,
keep a house and
a career.
I will teach my daughter
how to
laugh with life,
make tomato sauce and
step wildly into
this world.
I will teach my daughter
all i was never taught.

— I will be a good mother

We dig our toes in the dirt to
feel at home
tend the land, our gardens, wherever we roam,
flowers grow beneath our steps and the rivers
run clear of any impurities and all the fear,
like nature we can't tame a wild soul, but
with care, we can watch it grow.

I'll chop wood
and I'll haul water.

I'll continue to stoke the fire of my home,
heart.
To allow my passions to burn through my soul until they are
flaming outside of me.

When the moon is full I'll,
talk to her, whisper sweet words.

Days where the sun shines I'll,
laugh more, out of this belly.

Clouded skies will remind me,
to look for life in peculiar places.

When my hand falls on your hide
I understand the immensity of your life,
and all that was given to feed my own.

The way the sun dances as it hits the January
snow, reminds me,
of the mobility of life and to simply
go with the flow

How false life is with
pixels between our
hands,
don't you see the
dust collecting on
your plant stands
or the floorboards
aging without the
squeak of sneaking
out.
Your days are passing while
cobwebs collect in the
spaces of your fingers
and weeds pop through
the cracks of your drive
one day the
sun will set
and never rise again,
oh the pain in the memories
you have missed while
staring at box
between your fingertips

It's been 8 years and i've learned to move forward,
a tragedy once has shaped me and who i am
today.
I drink in life and listen to the birds,
watch my children play,
one bears your name,
although sadness clouds my heart from
time to time,
I've learned how to make it on just fine.

I've slowly come to
accept that i am
not one to have a
big circle of friends.
I live too far out of
town to be invited
to events or visited
very often.
Nobody just 'drops by'
like they used to.
But i suppose that's okay,
I have my kids, a husband
who loves me and
I've learnt to love me too.

cheryl floris

6 months has
gone by since we
almost lost you.
The memories of
you laying in
the hospital
bed are still
burned into my
head,
a picture i can't
erase.
But the woman
who has replaced
the one you were
feels like the *you*est
you've ever been
since dad died,
and i am happy
to see a twinkle in
your eye,
hear laughter
pour from your
mouth.
I recognize this
woman as the
mother I once had,

I hope she's here to stay.

I open my eyes
And life is a lot
different now.
Healing has been
had, the breath
of pain released.
I finally feel my
shoulders fall away
from my ears.
Theres been 8
years of hurt
and heartbreak,
this is the first
that feels like an
end to it all.
Maybe we can be
whole again.

who *death* made me

Instead of my daughter wrapping her arms around you
she stands on top, 8 feet deep
returned to earth your body is
somewhere else your soul has gone
and while I miss you dearly,
I became who I was meant to be, when you left me
for that I am grateful,
and I will continue to see your light and live by your words
in that, you will forever be alive.

who *death* made me

cheryl floris

DAD, what was your toughest lesson in life?

Take care of the ones you love.
be it siblings, your wife or
your family, or your friends
One day you may lose them.
Do whatever you can to prevent
that from happening.

Death has no return policy.

—Al Tudhope 1958 - 2014

who *death* made me

cheryl floris

For my father and mother, if I can write about the pain
and moments of suffering, I can write about the love
and happiness too.

You shaped me into the person I am today, you showed
me how to fill my life with nothing but what brings me
joy. I love you both.

For my husband,
I will love you endlessly.

who *death* made me

about the book

who death made me is the journey of healing from heartbreak that death caused. These poems and prose are a compilation of the unravelling of self once the passing of a loved one has raked your life. There is separation, dismantling and loneliness, there is grief and times where we try to fill the void that is left. There is loss in a multitude of ways, and I don't think anyone can anticipate that until they've gotten lost in the dead forest.

The writings in this book are the piecing back together of self and relationships, of diverging onto a path of alignment and truth, uncovering the ugly parts and covering them in earth to grow into beautiful things.

And they have,
There are flowers sprouting through me,
Grass growing under my feet,
Love and appreciation in the new stages of relationship with all of my loved ones.

I hope you can find the resilience to heal,
Life becomes beautiful once again.

who *death* made me

Manufactured by Amazon.ca
Bolton, ON